MARKETING CHILDREN'S BOOKS FOR INTROVERTS

A Practical Guide to Digital Marketing

Diana Aleksandrova

CONTENTS

INTRODUCTION   1

TARGET AUDIENCE AND MOTIVATION   7

Chapter 1 Narrowing Down Your Target Audience   9

Chapter 2 What is Your Book Really About?   13

Chapter 3 Motivation For Buying   15

Chapter 4 Crafting Your Message   22

Chapter 5 Customer Persona   25

BUILDING AN ONLINE PRESENCE   37

Chapter 6 Creating Your Website   39

Chapter 7 Leveraging SEO   41

Chapter 8 Author Profiles   43

Chapter 9 Setting Up Your Social Media Accounts   47

SPREAD THE WORD   51

Chapter 10 Social Media Strategy   53

Chapter 11 Picking The Right Influencer   57

Chapter 12 Collaborating With Influencers   62

Chapter 13 Measuring Success and Continuing The Relationship 66

Chapter 14 Participating In Virtual Book Tours   69

Chapter 15 Press Releases   71

Chapter 16 Marketing Materials   78

SALES AND RETENTION   81

Chapter 17 Amazon   83

Chapter 18 Paid Advertising   88

Chapter 19 Email List   101

Chapter 20 Email Automation and Segmentation   103

Chapter 21 Reviews   106

Chapter 22 A Word on Book Awards   115

REFLECTION   117

Chapter 23 My Mistakes   119

Chapter 24 Avoid Burnout   123

RESOURCES   127

INTRODUCTION

"DREAM BIG. START SMALL. ACT NOW."

There was a time when I believed that publishing my first children's book would bring in enough money for me to quit my full-time job. Needless to say, it didn't happen quite that way. The road to profitable publishing was filled with trials, errors, slipups, and setbacks. I took numerous classes, attended conferences, and even paid others to manage different aspects of my marketing efforts. The results were inconsistent and minimal. Let's say they were pretty proportional to my efforts. I knew I had to get serious if I wanted to succeed.

Learning from others was beneficial, but I soon realized that all those successful authors had something in common: they were very active at book readings, library signings, and other in-person events. Many of them made the majority of their income from school visits.

Most classes and lectures I attended emphasized the importance of getting reading engagements, selling at in-person events, attending book fairs, giving interviews, and creating interest in my books through face-to-face interactions.

There was a problem with that. I wasn't willing to do in-person events. As an introvert, the thought of standing in front of a room full of kids staring at me made me grit my teeth and sweat simultaneously. On one occasion, I even refused an interview over Zoom. Public speaking terrified me, and socializing with strangers always felt awkward. No matter how many people told me I had to overcome my fears and embrace the uncomfortable situations that would make me grow, I didn't want to do readings and signings. It wasn't about growing but truly enjoying what I did. A little voice in my head also told me I could do it my way. Instead of trying to overcome my introversion, I embraced another challenge: finding a way to sell children's books successfully from my desk. I had to learn what worked for me: *the introverted author!*

Here's the truth: my friends have always been my biggest cheerleaders, showing more pride and faith in my writing than I ever did. It's not that I doubted the quality of my books. I knew they were well-accepted by everyone who saw them and loved by kids, parents, and teachers. But talking about myself or my accomplishments made my cheeks burn with embarrassment. Still, if I wanted to sell books, I had to step out of my cozy shell and showcase them to the world. After all, no one can buy something they don't know exists.

Fortunately, in today's tech-savvy world, most people spend more time glued to their phones, scrolling through endless streams of content, than talking to other humans face-to-face. *This is the golden age of digital marketing!* It allows introverts like you and me to connect with potential readers and sell our books without the terrifying prospect of in-person interactions.

All we need is a strategy, a plan, and some discipline.

It takes time to build an author's platform and even more time to notice a significant result from your marketing. Each action builds on the previous one, and the effect compounds over time, gradually creating momentum that turns small efforts into measurable success.

Creating a comprehensive digital marketing plan for a children's book involves addressing each stage of the marketing funnel: *awareness, interest and consideration, conversion,* and *retention.*

Awareness: Increase visibility and reach to potential readers and their parents. Make sure your book reaches your potential readers.

Interest and Consideration: Engage potential customers and build interest in the book. Craft a message that speaks to them. Nurture leads and convince them of the book's value.

Conversion: Convert interested individuals into customers. Make it easy for customers to buy your book.

Retention: Create that relationship that will sell the next book.

I've separated this process into a few steps—each with a designated section—which you can easily refer to later:

I.   Target audience, motivation, and message.

II.   Building an online presence.

III.   Spread the word.

IV.   Sales and Retention.

V.   Reflection.

Downloadable templates and resources on writing, publishing, and marketing:

https://www.dedonibooks.com/resources

Ready?

Let's go!

TARGET AUDIENCE AND MOTIVATION

Knowing your book and your intended audience is essential. Understanding your book involves recognizing all its selling points and finding its unique value. At the same time, knowing your target customers' needs and motivation allows you to connect with them successfully.

8

Chapter 1 Narrowing Down Your Target Audience

Before you begin your marketing efforts, you need to know your target audience.

Not knowing your audience and not having a strategy and plan will cost you a lot of money and have minimal (if any) results. Trust me, I have done that. Throwing spaghetti on the wall and hoping something sticks is not a strategy that works here.

The main reason to target your marketing efforts is that you are not a big corporation with an unlimited budget. You cannot afford to waste your limited resources on ads showing your book to people with zero interest in purchasing it.

Children's books are a little tricky because the ones they are intended for are not the ones buying them. You have to appeal not only to the children but also to the person buying the book: the parent, the teacher, etc.

The classic way is to conduct research by talking to potential customers, sending surveys, and conducting polls. The good news is that you no longer have to do that. You can if you want, but reading reviews from real customers online is an easy way to obtain all the information you need. Reviews can be a treasure trove for you as a digital marketer. *Why conduct surveys when people leave their thoughts and opinions freely online?* Go to the reviews section for books similar to yours and read what everyone has to say.

Here is some of the information to consider when trying to figure out your target audience:

Demographics: Identify the age groups you want to write for, then figure out and chart their demographic characteristics, interests, and reading levels. *Do you have a board, picture, chapter, or middle-grade book?*

Popular Genres and Themes: Research which genres and themes are popular among your target age group. Look at bestseller lists, review sites, and book fairs to see what types of books are in demand. *What categories does your book fall into?* Amazon and Goodreads are great places to begin. Visit

Target and Barnes & Noble and take note of what dominates the shelves.

Competitor Analysis: Study successful authors and publishers within your genre. Analyze their books, marketing strategies, and audience engagement to learn what works well in the market. Look for similar books to yours. Read through the reviews and evaluate them. Follow those authors on social media and determine what they are doing right.

Do you have a niche? Identify potential niches in which your books can be placed. My best-performing book is *I Will Be There*, a story dedicated to all fathers. Even though I have a book about moms, which is a much bigger market, my father's book sells much better.

The more you narrow down your niche, the more effort and resources you can use to target that audience, which, if chosen right, will be the most interested in your book.

One example of narrowing down a niche is my *Dino Trouble* series targeting method.

Dino Trouble is a chapter book series, more specifically, an early chapter book series. It is easy to follow and read and has illustrations on every page. Because of that, I market it to parents with reluctant readers at home.

Children's Books – Chapter Books – Early Chapter Books – Reluctant Readers

You can see how I narrowed it down. It is not an overcrowded market and doesn't exclude kids who love reading either. Always think of unique ways to define and market your book.

Finding a niche can be gold.

Chapter 2 What is Your Book Really About?

Does your book teach a valuable lesson? Does it help children overcome fears or develop skills?

Authors know their stories best.

Yet, others can surprise you with a different take on your story that you hadn't thought of. Sometimes, authors are too close to their own stories and need an outside perspective to grasp the many different aspects of their own words fully.

I wrote *Too Cute to Spook*, focusing on making it about being different, acceptance, and growth.

After finishing the book, I tried to write a blurb, focusing on being different and accepting one's shortcomings.

However, many reviews indicated that the book helped their kids overcome their fear of monsters or go to sleep alone. Also, it became a best seller in October, and I never meant for it to be a Halloween book—but apparently, all monster books are. *Too Cute to Spook* started as a story of acceptance and finding one unique strength. It became a best-selling Halloween book and a way for kids to defeat their fears. You see, one book can serve many purposes, and oftentimes, we, the authors, are too close to the story to see all the possibilities.

Ask other authors, friends, or family to read your story and share their take on it with you. You will gain valuable feedback that will help you in crafting your blurbs.

Think about out-of-the-box ways your book can enhance your readers' lives. There is always more than one way to describe a book. You will be surprised by how others find different meanings in your book (reading the reviews helps with that, too).

Chapter 3 Motivation For Buying

Why do people buy children's books?

In the digital age, where screens dominate much of children's entertainment, parents look for more than just stories in the books they purchase for their kids. Books are tools for education, bonding, and nurturing creativity. Understanding the motivations behind why parents buy children's books and the problems these books solve can help marketers craft compelling messages to increase sales.

Surface motivations

On the surface, here are some of the motivations for buying children's books:

Educational Value: Books can introduce children to new words, improve their comprehension skills, and provide knowledge about the world. That is why STEAM (science, technology, engineering, arts, and math) books have become so popular recently.

Reading cultivates empathy and emotional intelligence. If you give kids characters they relate to, they will feel with them. If you give them the ones they like, they will cheer for them. If you provide them with a villain, they will learn what is wrong and what is right.

Reading helps kids develop their cognitive powers and improve their *reasoning and intelligence*, allowing them to accomplish more in life.
Reading develops kids' *imagination and creative thinking*, which improves problem-solving abilities.

Books expand kids' world beyond their immediate surroundings. They provide them with experiences they cannot encounter in person. It can expose them to different cultures, places, obstacles, and characters. The variety opens up their horizons.

Reading teaches kids values. The easiest way to learn is while having fun. Kids learn best by example. If you give children someone they admire, they will follow their example.

Reading sparks curiosity and opens up kids' minds to all possibilities, which in turn is how inventors and discoverers are shaped.

Books that can create great memories encourage asking questions and encourage interaction, which helps strengthen the relationship between a parent and a child.

Many parents strive to instill a love for reading from an early age. They know that children who enjoy reading are more likely to succeed academically and maintain a lifelong habit of reading. Engaging, fun, and age-appropriate books are essential to achieving this goal.

Problems Solved by Children's Books

Screen Time Management: One of the significant challenges parents face today is managing their children's screen time. Children's books provide an excellent alternative to electronic devices, offering an engaging way to entertain and educate without the need for screens.

Attention Span Development: With the rapid pace of digital content, children's attention spans are often short. Reading books helps develop longer attention spans and patience as children learn to follow a story from beginning to end.

Preparation for School: Parents often worry about their children being prepared for school. Children's books that cover basic skills such as counting, letters, shapes, and social skills can ease this concern, helping children to be school-ready.

Reading improves vocabulary and one's ability to express oneself. This helps with communication and leads to better test scores.

Addressing Behavioral Issues: Many children's books address common behavioral issues, such as sharing, manners, and bedtime routines. These books can be helpful tools for parents to reinforce positive behavior and address challenges in a relatable way for children.

Providing Diverse Perspectives: In an increasingly diverse world, parents look for books that reflect different cultures, backgrounds, and experiences. Books that offer diverse perspectives can help children understand and appreciate the world beyond their immediate environment.

As I mentioned before, those are motivations for purchasing children's books on the surface. But let's dive deeper into what stands behind those motivations. *What is the deeper motivation for parents to buy children's books?*

Deeper Motivations (human nature)

Buying children's books is often driven by more profound, more intrinsic motivations that go beyond the surface-level benefits of education, bonding, and entertainment. While parents certainly aim to be good caregivers, purchasing children's books taps into a range of psychological and emotional desires that shape their behavior and decisions that go beyond good parenting. Understanding these deeper motivations can provide better insights for marketers and educators alike.

Self-Validation and Identity: There are set expectations of what it means to be a good parent. Selecting, purchasing, and reading books to their children allows parents to affirm their identity as nurturing, responsible, and engaged caregivers. At a fundamental level, many parents buy children's books as a form of self-validation. By investing in books, parents often feel they are fulfilling an essential part of their role, reinforcing their self-esteem and sense of purpose.

Creating a Legacy: Parents often see books as an investment in their children's future. Buying books is seen as creating a legacy, a way to pass down knowledge and values. This desire to make a lasting impact is a powerful motivator, driven by the need to contribute positively to their child's life journey.

Fear of failure: Parenting is full of uncertainties and anxieties about the future. Books offer a tangible way for parents to feel they are taking proactive steps in their child's development. Books provide a sense of control and reassurance, whether it's about preparing their child for school, addressing behavioral issues, or simply providing wholesome entertainment. This helps alleviate the anxieties of raising a child in an unpredictable world.

Social and Cultural Pressure: There is also a social and cultural dimension to buying children's books. In many communities, there is an unspoken pressure to meet specific parenting standards, often including having a well-stocked library for children. Parents may feel compelled to buy books to meet these societal expectations and to be seen as informed and conscientious parents by their peers.

Pride: Parents feel proud when their children achieve developmental milestones, such as learning to read, expanding their vocabulary, or understanding complex concepts. Books are tools that help children reach these milestones, thus reinforcing parental pride.

Guilt: Nowadays, most families have two working parents, and many consist of one single parent. Parents feel guilt for not having enough time to spend with their children. Buying books makes them feel like they are spending money on something that will benefit their kids.

Understanding these deeper motivations can significantly boost your marketing strategies for children's books.

Chapter 4 Crafting Your Message

Understanding parents' motivations and challenges can help you position your children's books not just as a product but as an essential tool for a child's growth, happiness, and success.

Highlight how books contribute to a child's future success and well-being, reinforcing the idea of creating a lasting legacy. Use storytelling in marketing materials that showcase the emotional bonds and cherished memories formed through reading together. Provide reassurance through messaging that emphasizes the developmental benefits of reading and how books can help address common parental concerns. Leverage testimonials and endorsements from other parents to create a sense of community and shared values around reading.

Different ways to craft your message

Highlight Educational Benefits: Emphasize how the book aids in learning and development. Use testimonials from educators and parents to reinforce the educational value.

Create Emotional Connections: Share stories and images of parents and children bonding over books. Highlight the emotional and relational benefits of reading together.

Showcase Creativity and Fun: Use vibrant visuals and engaging content to showcase the imaginative and fun aspects of your book.

Address Parental Concerns: Use marketing messages that address common parental concerns, such as reducing screen time and preparing for school. Provide evidence or endorsements that support these claims.

By tapping into the deeper motivations, you can create more resonant and effective campaigns that connect with parents emotionally, driving sales and loyalty. You will do best if you remember both the "surface" and the "deeper" motivations when creating your message.

Here are some phrases that target both motivations:
Invest in your child's future.
Nurture their potential.
Champion their growth.

Foster a bright future.

Guide their educational journey.

Inspire their dreams.

Shape their intellectual growth.

Of course, no two books are the same, and you need to find your unique selling point and create an offer your customer cannot refuse. Stress on benefits over features. How would your book help your target audience?

Chapter 5 Customer Persona

So, who is your target audience?

After *researching,* you should know your target audience and their motivation for buying children's books. *Is it a parent or grandparent of a child interested in martial arts? Or maybe a biology or music teacher?* The more specific you are in determining your target audience, the more tailored and successful your marketing campaign will be.

A customer persona represents your ideal customer based on your research. It helps you understand your customers' preferences and needs, which allows you to create a more effective marketing strategy.

You can design one or a few customer personas for each target audience you identify.

Following are two examples of customer personas for *Dino Trouble.* The first is for a mother of a reluctant reader, and the second is for teachers who recommend the book to kids struggling with reading.

Customer Persona 1

Name: Mom of eight-year-old Monica

Age: 36 years old

Gender: Female

Location: USA

Goals:

Encourage Monica to develop a love for reading.

Find educational and engaging content that can hold Monica's interest.

Support Monica's academic and personal growth.

Challenges:

Balancing work and family time

Ensuring Monica finds reading materials that are both appealing and age-appropriate

Overcoming Monica's resistance to traditional reading

Buying Habits:

Prefers recommendations from teachers, librarians, and online reviews

Look for books that have educational value but are also fun and engaging

Willing to invest in books that promise to keep Monica interested and help improve her reading skills

Marketing Message: "Foster a love for reading with our engaging chapter books designed for reluctant readers. Our books combine a healthy blend of humor and shivers that keep kids turning the pages, making reading fun."

By addressing both personas, marketers can effectively target the needs and motivations of the parent, who makes the purchase decision, and the child, who ultimately uses the product.

Customer Persona 2

Name: Ms. Teacher

Age: 40 years old

Gender: Female

Occupation: Fifth Grade Teacher

Classroom Environment:

A diverse group of students with varying reading levels and interests

Incorporates a mix of traditional and modern teaching methods

Emphasizes a supportive and inclusive learning environment

Goals:

Improve students' reading skills and comprehension.

Foster a love for reading among students, especially those who struggle with it.

Provide resources that cater to different learning styles and reading levels.

Challenges:

Limited classroom resources and budget constraints

Keeping struggling readers engaged and motivated

Finding books that are both educational and enjoyable for reluctant readers

Preferred Book Features:

Short, manageable chapters that maintain students' interest

Books with plenty of illustrations and visual aids to support understanding

Interactive elements like quizzes, discussion questions, or activities related to the story

Relatable characters and engaging age-appropriate plots

Themes that resonate with students' interests and experiences

Teaching Strategies:

Use read-aloud sessions to model fluent reading and engage students.

Incorporate group discussions and activities related to the book to enhance comprehension.

Provide individualized reading support and encouragement to struggling readers.

Motivations:

Passionate about helping students develop lifelong reading habits

Seeks out innovative and effective teaching resources

Enjoys seeing students make progress and gain confidence in their reading abilities

Marketing Message:

"Empower your students to become confident readers with our engaging chapter books designed for reluctant readers. Our books feature captivating stories with humorous illustrations on every page, making reading a fun and rewarding experience. Perfect for classroom use, these books will help your students develop the skills and love for reading that will last a lifetime."

Creating customer personas can help you craft and tailor your message. Try making some for your books. They don't have to include all the information from the examples above. You will build upon them over time. Reading the reviews of books similar to yours will tell you what readers find helpful in the stories. It will show you their needs and motivations for buying the product.

We are lucky to live in the digital era, where everything is easily accessible, even customers' thoughts and preferences.

Today, you don't have to send out surveys and wait for people to fill them out and return them to you. You can access all that from the comfort of your chair.

Customer Persona 1

Relationship to the child:

_____

Child's interests:

_____

_____

_____

Child's struggles:

_____

_____

_____

Customer's goals:

_____

_____

_____

Customer's challenges:

_____

_____

_____

Where do they get their recommendations from? Where do they shop?

_____

_____

_____

Preferred book features:

_____

_____

_____

Other important information:

_____

_____

_____

Now try creating your marketing message for that customer:

_____

_____

_____

_____

_____

_____

_____

_____

_____

_____

_____

_____

_____

_____

_____

_____

_____

_____

_____

Customer Persona 2

Relationship to the child:

_____

Child's interests:

_____

_____

_____

Child's struggles:

_____

_____

_____

Customer's goals:

_____

_____

_____

Customer's challenges:

_____

_____

_____

Where do they get their recommendations from? Where do they shop?

_____

_____

_____

Preferred book features:

_____

_____

_____

Other important information:

_____

_____

_____

_____

Marketing message for that customer:

_____

_____

_____

_____

_____

_____

_____

_____

_____

_____

_____

_____

You can create as many as you need, but I recommend beginning with at least two different customer personas. This exercise will help you develop other ideas for your marketing messages.

You can download the Customer Persona template from: https://www.dedonibooks.com/resources

BUILDING AN ONLINE PRESENCE

In today's digital age, having a solid online presence is essential for any author, particularly for introverts. The internet offers numerous platforms for connecting with readers without the need for face-to-face interaction. Creating a website, blog, or social media account is a great way to begin building your online presence and marketing your children's books.

Chapter 6 Creating Your Website

A professional website serves as your online home base. Many people put all their efforts into designing their website with their brand colors and aesthetics in mind. An eye-catching website is all good until you can't find what you are looking for. Website functionality should be your number one priority. You want your customers to be able to find what they are looking for easily and quickly.

Here are some key elements to include:

About Me: Share your journey, your passion for writing, and what inspired you to write children's books.

Books: Showcase your published works with engaging descriptions, cover images, and links to purchase them.

Blog: This is not mandatory, but it can help build your credibility and SEO.

Contact Information: Make it easy for readers and potential collaborators to contact you.

Newsletter Sign-Up Form: Ideally, you will invite them to sign up for your newsletter at least three times. Use pop-up forms and embedded sign-up forms. Be very clear about what they will get by signing in. Generic "Let's Keep in Touch" does not have the power of "SUBSCRIBE TO MY NEWSLETTER AND RECEIVE FIVE WEEKS OF MARVELOUS SURPRISES, BEGINNING WITH A FREE BOOK!" You have to deliver what you promise. More on email marketing and newsletters later on.

Press Kit (Media Kit): This should be a page or document containing all the relevant information easily accessible to journalists or influencers.

Social Media Links: Make it easy for visitors to find your Social Media accounts.

Chapter 7 Leveraging SEO

Search Engine Optimization (SEO) is crucial for making your website discoverable. Here are some tips for improving your site's SEO and making Google your new best friend.

Keywords: Use relevant keywords throughout your site, especially in titles and headings. For children's books, keywords like "children's book author," "kids' stories," and "educational books for children" can be effective. Just don't go overboard.

Quality Content: You cannot just stuff your website with keywords. You need quality content. Update your blog regularly with high-quality, engaging content. This attracts readers and signals to search engines that your site is active and relevant.

Clear structure: None of the above matters if your quality content cannot be found. Organizing your website in a user-friendly way helps visitors and search engines alike discover your content.

Give each page a title: Each page needs to have a title.

Descriptions: Besides giving each page a title, write compelling descriptions with relevant keywords. These summaries appear in search engine results and can entice users to click on your site.

Proper Linking: Link your pages, making your site easy to navigate and easy for search engines to crawl.

Optimizing your website's SEO will improve its visibility on search engine result pages and increase traffic.

Chapter 8 Author Profiles

Goodreads

Goodreads is an invaluable platform for connecting with your audience, gathering reviews, and promoting your books. Think of Goodreads as a giant virtual book club, where everyone discusses their latest reads, shares recommendations, and adds to their ever-growing "to-be-read" lists.

Create a profile to showcase your books. Interact with your readers by participating in _Ask the Author_ to build a connection. You can also connect your blog to your author profile. The platform offers the option of participating in giveaways and promoting your books.

Goodreads is where book lovers are. Even if you don't go through the extra effort of running promotions and doing giveaways, include a bio and a link to your website—make it easy for readers to find you.

Another way to connect with the community of readers on Goodreads is to share your reading preferences and recommend books you enjoy. That way, you can connect with readers who share your interests and create a genuine connection. Also, by recommending your fellow authors' books, you become a part of a tribe that can help you succeed. Your fellow authors are your peers and can be your biggest supporters.

Recently, Amazon began showing Goodreads rankings along with the Amazon rankings. Goodreads reviews have more merit to buyers since they are exclusively by actual readers.

Amazon Author Central

Creating your profile on Amazon Author Central is a must. Not only can readers read your bio (in more than one language) and see all your books in one place, but they can also follow you and be notified about your new releases.

This is a great place to check your Amazon ranking, change your book description, recommend similar books, and even include notes with your book. You can also check your weekly sales and all the reviews your books have received, all in one place.

Amazon is constantly making improvements, and Amazon Author Central is evolving continually. It is already connected to Amazon Advertising, and you can be redirected to the ads console with one click. *Why is this important?* In the past, you could run ads for books published only through KDP. This is no longer the case. You can now run ads for all books under your Author Central Profile. Some changes aren't that great, though. Since November 2023, graphics and videos are not displayed on Author Pages. That was an excellent opportunity to showcase your book trailers, but it is no longer available.

You can have up to three pen names under one Author Central account.

BookBub, BookLife, Reedsy Discovery, and *SCBWI* (Society of Children's Book Writers and Illustrators) are other platforms where you can create an author profile.

Do not get overwhelmed trying to create a profile at each platform that offers the option. The most important ones are Amazon and Goodreads.

Chapter 9 Setting Up Your Social Media Accounts

Everyone is on social media nowadays. Okay, almost everyone. But the majority of your potential customers are on social media, and it's probably a good idea for you to be where they hang out, too. Social media allows you to engage and build relationships for free, showcase and promote your books, and gain a faithful following.

Choosing the Right Platforms

First things first, you don't need to be everywhere at once. Pick a few platforms that best suit your audience and your style. Here's a quick rundown of the most popular ones:

Facebook is great for reaching parents and educators.

Instagram is perfect for sharing eye-catching book covers, illustrations, and behind-the-scenes shots. Reels are gaining more traction and replacing graphics and pictures.

Twitter(X) is ideal for short, snappy updates and engaging in conversations. I am not a fan of that one, but many parents hang out there.

Pinterest is fantastic for sharing educational content and activities. It's like a giant, virtual scrapbooking party where everyone looks for inspiration and cool DIY projects.

TikTok is the place for creative, short videos showcasing your personality and books.

YouTube is for read-alouds, animated book trailers, and demonstrations.

Don't try to be everywhere unless you love social media. Focus your efforts where your audience is and on the platform you feel comfortable with.

Set Up Linktree

Linktree (https://linktr.ee) is a popular online tool that allows you to create a single link containing multiple destinations, which you can place in your social media bios, like on Instagram or Twitter. Instead of choosing just one link to share with your audience, Linktree lets you set up a simple, customizable landing page with buttons that direct users to various links, such as your website, book sales pages, newsletter sign-up, social media profiles, and more. They offer free and paid versions and provide basic analytics.

SPREAD THE WORD

No one can buy a book they haven't heard of.

For your book to succeed, people need to know it exists.

Chapter 10 Social Media Strategy

Once you've chosen your platforms, it's time to get strategic. Here's how to craft a plan that's as effective as it is entertaining:

Plan and schedule: Plan, create, and schedule your posts in advance. Planning helps you stay organized and consistent. Plus, it prevents those *"Oh no, what do I post today?"* moments.

Mix It Up: Vary your content to keep things interesting. Share book updates, personal anecdotes, behind-the-scenes looks, and fun activities for kids.
Download 35 Social Media Post Ideas if you need a little inspiration. https://www.dedonibooks.com/resources

Engage: Don't just post and ghost. Engage with your followers by responding to comments, participating in discussions, and asking questions. Engage with other accounts by commenting and sharing their content if they fit your niche and vision.

Hashtags: Use relevant hashtags to increase your reach. Popular ones for children's books include #KidLit, #ChildrensBooks, #Bookstagram, and #AmWriting. Experiment with different hashtags and see what gains traction. Hashtag stuffing doesn't guarantee more exposure. In my experience, using fewer, properly selected hashtags is more effective than adding all thirty allowed.

Mix up different media: Mix up posts with reels and stories. If you are not camera-shy (like me), you can go live or record yourself talking about relevant topics. People like to see the face behind the message, but that is not always necessary. You can put together videos in Canva and add a voice-over—yours or someone else's. For a higher engagement, include interactive posts. Ask questions, run polls, and encourage followers to share their thoughts and experiences.

Boost your most successful content: it might seem pointless to boost content already seen by many people, but there is a valid reason to do so. Boosting your best content allows it to be seen by people who are not your followers *yet*. This is the fastest way to reach more people and *gain more followers*.

Building a Community

One of the best things about social media is the sense of community it can create. Here's how to build a loyal following of readers and fans:

Consistency: Post regularly to keep your audience engaged.

Authenticity: Be yourself—people connect with authentic, relatable content.

Collaboration: Partner with other authors, illustrators, or influencers to cross-promote and reach new audiences.

Exclusive Content: Offer your followers something special, like sneak peeks, exclusive discounts, or early access to new releases.

Measuring Success

You'll need to measure your success to know if your social media efforts are paying off. Here are some metrics to keep an eye on:

Engagement: Track likes, comments, shares, and other interactions. High engagement means your content is resonating with your audience.

Reach: Look at how many people are seeing your posts. The more eyes on your content, the better.

Growth: Monitor your follower count and see how it changes over time. Growing your audience means you're doing something right.

Conversions: Track the number of people clicking on links to your website or purchasing your books. Linktree allows you to include more links and track the number of people who click on each one.

Social media is a great tool for children's book authors. It offers a way to connect with readers, promote books, and build a community. You can turn your social media presence into a powerful connection with your customers by choosing the right platforms, crafting a solid strategy, creating engaging content, and measuring your success.

Chapter 11 Picking The Right Influencer

Like any other business, children's book authors are increasingly turning to influencers. Influencers can be a powerful ally in expanding your following and reaching new readers. Picked right, influencers can even give your book credibility. Whether they're book bloggers, social media stars, or educational content creators, working with influencers can significantly boost your marketing efforts.

Understanding the Role of Influencers

Influencers are individuals with a substantial following on social media or other online platforms. They can sway their audience's opinions and purchasing decisions through their content. In the context of children's books, influencers can be parents, teachers, librarians, or even fellow authors who have built a reputation for recommending high-quality children's literature.

When it comes to social media influencers, more is not always best. More followers don't always mean more exposure and engagement. When researching influencers, don't just look at the number of followers but check out their engagement and the type of followers they have.

Engagement is likes, comments, and shares. Sadly, many "influencers" have what they call "fake followers." For a minimum amount, everyone can obtain thousands of followers who are not real people. They can also purchase likes for their posts. I have been contacted by accounts (more than one) with a million followers asking me to post about my book for a fee. An authentic influencer with a million followers would not be hustling collaboration for a minimum fee.

I have found that the most reliable engagement indicator is the number of comments. Look at the substance of the comments and the people posting them to check if they are from followers, part of your target audience, or a part of an engagement pod.

Are the comments always from the same accounts?

Are those commenting in the same business?

Are the comments quite identical? "That looks great," "Such a cute book," and "I love that." These generic responses indicate that the account participates in an engagement pod. These are influencers who comment on each other's posts to boost visibility.

Check out some of the followers, too. Fake accounts are also easy to identify—they usually follow thousands of accounts but have no meaningful posts and no followers.

Type of influencers by followers' count:

Nano Influencers – 1-10k followers

Micro-Influencers – 10-100k followers

Macro Influencers – 100k-1 Million followers

Mega Influencers – 1 Million+ followers

As a small business with a small budget, you should seek collaborations with Nano and Micro-influencers. Those influencers are not famous; they build their brand by posting exciting and authentic content and creating genuine relationships with their followers. They have a higher engagement rate than accounts with more followers and often specialize in different niches. Collaborating with an influencer specializing in the same niche as you (or the subject of your book) can be mutually beneficial, and that is how relationships are built.

The first step in working with influencers is identifying those who align with your brand and target audience. Here are some tips to help you find the right influencers:

Research: Look for influencers focusing on children's books, parenting, education, or related fields. Use social media platforms like Instagram, YouTube, TikTok, and Twitter to find potential collaborators.

Search for hashtags like *#TeacherPick, #ParentingTips, and #BookRecommendations*, or ones related to the subject of your book.

Audience Match: Ensure the influencer's audience matches your target demographic. Suppose you have a book about how to say "hello" in different languages and are trying to gauge which influencer might be a good fit. Look for influencers who travel with their kids. *Is their content family-friendly? Are their followers parents or educators, or are they young single women who like to travel solo?*

Engagement: Look for influencers with high engagement rates. An influencer with 10,000 followers and high engagement is often more valuable than one with 100,000 followers and low engagement. Engagement is more important than the number of followers.

Content Quality: Review their content to ensure it aligns with your brand's values and aesthetic. Look for influencers who produce high-quality, visually appealing, and authentic content.

Book Bloggers

Book bloggers are special influencers and can be important allies in promoting your children's books. Reach out to bloggers specializing in children's literature and ask if they would like to review your book. More on virtual book tours later on.

Chapter 12 Collaborating With Influencers

Approaching Influencers

Once you've identified potential influencers, the next step is to reach out to them. Here's how to do it effectively.

Personalized Outreach: Avoid generic messages. Instead, personalize your approach by mentioning specific things you like about their content and explaining why your book would fit their audience. Maybe your book aligns with a theme they're currently discussing, like back-to-school season or literacy month. Tailor your pitch to make it relevant to their audience.

A personalized message shows that you've done your homework and are genuinely interested in collaborating.

Clear Proposal: Be clear about what you're offering and what you're asking for in return. Whether you're offering a free copy of your book, a paid collaboration, or something else, make sure both parties understand the terms.

Highlight Benefits: Explain how the collaboration will benefit the influencer. *Will it provide valuable content for their audience? Will it offer them exclusive access to your work or other perks?*

Once an influencer agrees to collaborate, working together smoothly is important to ensure a successful partnership. Here's how to manage the collaboration process.

Provide Necessary Materials: Send the influencer a copy of your book, along with any additional materials they might need, such as press releases, high-resolution images, or promotional graphics.

Creative Freedom: Allow the influencer creative freedom to present your book in a way that resonates with their audience. Influencers know their followers best and have learned how to engage them effectively. I have never tried telling an influencer how to present my books.

Set Deadline or Posting Schedule: Clearly outline your expectations regarding the content, posting schedule, and any specific requirements you might have. Agree on deadlines and ensure both parties are on the same page.

Types of Influencer Collaborations

There are various ways to collaborate with influencers. Here are some popular types of collaborations that can effectively promote your children's books.

Book Reviews: Influencers can review your book on their blog, YouTube channel, or social media. A detailed, honest review can provide valuable exposure and build credibility for your book.

Giveaways: Hosting a giveaway in collaboration with an influencer can generate excitement and engagement. Ask the influencer to announce the giveaway, and encourage their followers to participate by liking, sharing, or commenting on the post.

Read-Alouds: Influencers can do read-aloud sessions of your book, either live or recorded. This can be especially engaging for children and parents looking for new books to read together. I love that type of collaboration. Most of the time, all I need to do is agree for them to read my book on their channel, and they use the Kindle version to create graphics.

Read-alouds do not bring many direct sales, but the exposure is priceless.

Guest Posts: Write a guest post for the influencer's blog or have them write one for yours. This can introduce your book to a new audience and provide valuable content for both platforms.

Social Media Takeovers: Allow the influencer to take over your social media accounts for a day. This can create a fun and engaging experience for your followers and attract the influencer's audience to your profiles. I am personally wary of this method, but I have to mention that it is an option here.

Chapter 13 Measuring Success and Continuing The Relationship

Measuring your influencer collaborations' success is essential to understanding their impact and refining your strategies. Here are some metrics to track:

Engagement: Look at likes, comments, shares, and other forms of engagement on the influencer's posts about your book. High engagement indicates that the content resonated with their audience.

Reach: Assess how many people were exposed to the influencer's content about your book. This includes views on videos, impressions on social media posts, and page visits on blog posts. Some metrics are public; the influencer can provide others.

Conversions: Track any increase in book sales, website traffic, or social media followers that can be attributed to the influencer collaboration.

Feedback: Pay attention to the feedback from the influencer's audience. Positive comments and reviews can be a good indicator of the collaboration's success.

Building Long-Term Relationships

Building long-term relationships with influencers can be highly beneficial. I have a good working relationship with a few influencers. They know that I contact them whenever I publish a new book, and they are always happy to collaborate with me.

Here's how to nurture these relationships:

Show Appreciation: Thank the influencers for their collaboration and acknowledge their effort publicly. A shoutout on your social media or a thank-you note can go a long way.

Stay Connected: Keep in touch with influencers even after the collaboration. Engage with their content and stay updated on their work. Building a genuine relationship can lead to future collaborations. Think of it as maintaining a friendship—don't be that person who only calls when they need a favor.

Offer Exclusives: Provide influencers with exclusive content or early access to your new books. This will make them feel valued and give them unique content to share with their audience.

Working with influencers can be a game-changer in promoting your children's books. You can tap into their engaged audiences and amplify your reach by identifying the right influencers, approaching them effectively, and managing the collaboration smoothly. Remember to measure the success of your collaborations and build long-term relationships with influencers to maximize their impact.

Chapter 14 Participating In Virtual Book Tours

Virtual book tours are an excellent way to reach a wider audience without leaving the comfort of your home. Your book will be featured on the different blog sites each day. There are virtual blog tour companies that offer the service for a fee. Instead of you approaching each blogger or influencer, they handle all the communication and the scheduling for you.

When choosing a virtual book tour managing company, ask about the bloggers they work with. Make sure those have the right audience. There is no point in spending resources to show your book on a blog whose primary readers are into science fiction or romance.

Plan Ahead: Schedule your tour around your book's release date. Give yourself plenty of time to arrange dates with bloggers and influencers.

Diverse Content: Plan a variety of content for each stop on your tour. This could include interviews, guest posts, book reviews, and giveaways.

Promotion: Promote each tour stop on your social media and website. Encourage your readers to follow along and participate. It's like leading a parade—make it fun and everyone will join in.

Chapter 15 Press Releases

Getting the word out about your children's book with a press release can be a game-changer, but it takes a bit of strategy. First, you'll want to craft a press release that shines—think of it as your book's elevator pitch. Highlight what makes your book special, why readers will love it, and any exciting praise or endorsements it has received.

Once your press release is polished and ready to go, the next step is finding the right places to send it. This is where a little homework comes in handy. Look for magazines, newsletters, and websites that cater to your niche audience. These outlets already speak to your ideal audience and are more likely to be interested in your book. Research the editors responsible for the section your book might fit best and craft a personalized email.

By targeting your press release to these specific publications, you're not just casting a wide net and hoping for the best—you're strategically placing your book in front of people who are most likely to be excited about it.

Consider reaching out to local newspapers and community newsletters as well, especially if your book has regional or cultural significance. These publications often spotlight local authors and can be valuable resources for gaining support.

Don't just send your press release and hope for the best—follow up and build relationships with the media contacts you reach out to. Personalized emails can go a long way; mention why your book would be a great fit for their publication and offer to provide a review copy or do an interview. Establishing a rapport with journalists and bloggers can lead to ongoing opportunities for exposure, not just a one-time mention.

Paid Press Release Distribution Services

Send2Press and *Newswire* are two popular services that can help get your press release in front of a broad audience, including journalists, bloggers, and news outlets. These platforms have established networks and distribution channels that can give your children's book the exposure it needs.

When using paid press release distribution services like Send2Press or Newswire, it's important to ensure your press release follows their specific formatting guidelines to maximize its effectiveness and reach, which typically includes:

Headline: The headline should be clear, concise, and attention-grabbing. It should summarize the key points of your press release and entice the reader to learn more.

Sub-headline (Optional): A sub-headline provides additional detail that complements the headline, offering more context or highlighting an important aspect of your book.

Dateline: The dateline includes the release date and the city where the press release is issued. For example: "August 26, 2024, New York, NY –"

Introduction: The first paragraph should succinctly introduce your book, explaining what it is and why it's newsworthy. This is where you hook the reader with the most compelling aspects of your story.

Body: The body of the press release expands on the introduction. Include details about your book's plot, target audience, any unique features, and any awards or endorsements it has received. This section should be informative and engaging, with quotes or testimonials if available.

Contact Information: Provide your contact details, including your name, phone number, email address, and any relevant social media handles or website links. This allows journalists or interested parties to reach out for more information.

Boilerplate: A boilerplate is a short paragraph at the end of the press release providing background information about you as the author or your publishing company. It's a standardized "about us" section.

Following is my press release for *The Lazy Stork*, which was distributed through Send2Press.

Children's book author Diana Aleksandrova turns her struggles to become pregnant into children's book bringing solace and hope to others.

Las Vegas, Nevada, USA – Diana Aleksandrova has always wanted to be a mom, but after years of trying to become pregnant, that dream hasn't come true yet. Inspired by her struggles and the legend about the storks bringing the babies, she writes "The Lazy Stork" ISBN: 978-1-953118-26-4, May 2023.

In The Lazy Stork, Stan the Stork slept through most of his training, so his first delivery isn't as easy as he thought. When the compass makes him swirl in circles and he can't read the map, he is afraid his mission is a failure.

Despite the hardship that brought this book to life, The Lazy Stork is anything but sad. On the contrary, it is full of humor and hope.

THE STORY BEHIND THE STORY

"After years of suffering from infertility, I decided to blame it on 'the lazy stork.' I needed some humor in my life when everything seemed so dark. With a surprising happier-than-the-happiest of endings, The Lazy Stork is meant to bring hope to the families still waiting for their miracles. The story shows kids how much their parents wished, waited, and longed for them to arrive. It's a lighthearted and humorous way to explain why their baby brother or sister hasn't come yet. Blame it on the stork!"

Diana hopes to bring awareness to the fact that one in eight couples in the US are impacted by infertility! Infertility is not a condition that individuals choose or can prevent and there is little to no support for families affected by it. Diana lives in Nevada, a state that does not mandate fertility coverage, and most companies elect not to offer such.

ABOUT THE AUTHOR

Diana Aleksandrova is an award-winning author of children's books. Her mission is to help emerging and reluctant readers fall in love with books. Diana believes that reading is beneficial for children and is a way to shape the thinking of an emotionally intelligent future generation.

BOOK SUMMARY

Name: The Lazy Stork

Written by Diana Aleksandrova

Illustrated by Svilen Dimitrov

Hardcover ISBN: 978-1-953118-26-4

Paperback ISBN: 978-1-953118-27-1

Library of Congress Control Number: 2022916190

Preorder campaign: March 2023

Publication Date: May 1st, 2023

Publisher: Dedoni (https://www.dedonibooks.com)

Contact: dedonibooks@gmail.com

Video Trailer: https://youtu.be/O_Wl7_rwjww

Tips for Submission

Adhere to Word Count: Most services have a word count limit, typically around 400-800 words, so keep your press release concise and focused.

Use SEO Keywords: If the service offers SEO optimization, consider including relevant keywords that can help your press release rank higher in search engine results.

Include Links: Make sure to include hyperlinks to your book's sales page, your website, or social media profiles to make it easy for readers to find more information.

Proofread Thoroughly: A polished, error-free press release will reflect positively on you and your book.

A paid press release service can be beneficial for SEO purposes but rarely will garner more interviews or direct sales. For more targeted exposure, research publications interested in your genre or local publications.

Chapter 16 Marketing Materials

Creating marketing materials is time-consuming but can be fun at the same time. As a creative, you might enjoy the challenge or decide to delegate that part of your effort.

Canva has become an invaluable tool in my marketing journey. The website has a very user-friendly interface. You don't need technical knowledge to use its many features and become a pro in creating eye-catching graphics and reels.

You don't have to exhaust yourself trying to create separate graphics and videos for each platform you are on. Repurposing content is a smart and efficient way to maximize your marketing efforts across multiple platforms. For example, a blog post about the inspiration behind your children's book can be broken down into shorter social media posts, turned into an email newsletter, or used as the basis for a YouTube video. Similarly, quotes from your book can be turned into shareable graphics, and illustrations can be featured in Instagram stories or Pinterest boards. By adapting one piece of content for different platforms, you maintain consistency while reaching a broader audience without constantly creating new material.

For more complex materials like animated book trailers, you can find freelancers on Fiverr or Upwork. There are a lot of unethical freelancers on both platforms, so make sure you do your due diligence and vet the professionals you hire.

I love the versatile uses of book trailers, for example. Besides posting them on Social Media to garner organic engagement, you can include them on your website. Videos quickly capture the attention of visitors, and embedding the trailer on your book's landing page offers a visual preview that complements your written description. This improves the user experience and boosts the likelihood of turning visitors into readers. You can post your book trailer on your Amazon Product page. It will be shown just above the reviews. You can NOT mention Amazon directly in your video or show the Amazon name or logo in any way (or your video won't be approved; ask me. I learned the tough way).

Amazon has introduced a cool new feature allowing you to incorporate video into your Amazon Ads. Your book trailer can appear as part of Sponsored Brand Video ads, reaching potential readers directly on Amazon's platform. This type of ad is particularly effective because it allows you to capture attention in a highly relevant context, driving more qualified traffic to your book's page. To be eligible to be posted on Amazon as an ad, a video should be in the proper format and under 45 seconds.

SALES AND RETENTION

Sales are crucial for your book's success, but retention is what builds a loyal readership. To drive sales, make your book visible and accessible, and create an offer tailored to your target audience. Once a sale is made, keep readers engaged with exclusive content, updates, and sneak peeks of future projects. Encourage reviews and interactions to foster strong connections, turning readers into advocates who spread the word about your books.

Chapter 17 Amazon

Amazon is the largest bookshop in the world. That has its advantages as well as disadvantages. This is where people shop for the next read, but at the same time, it's hard to stand out among the millions of books there.

That is why you need to ensure that your book has the best chance of being noticed and convince potential customers that this is what they are looking for.

The first step is to show your book to as many people as possible.

The proper *metadata* is crucial for that.

Metadata is your book's title, subtitle, blurb, keywords, and categories. Picking the right keywords and writing a good description can help more people see your book. You should select high-demand, low-competition keywords to ensure your book appears first when customers search using those terms. Well-thought-out metadata will help your book reach its target audience, support marketing efforts, and drive more sales.

Amazon Advertising is another way to increase the visibility of your book.

The next step is to get potential buyers to click on your book.

This is where the cover and a catchy title come into play. I didn't realize how many people judge a book by its cover for real. Silly me always thought it was just a saying. And this is even more true when it comes to children's books since the illustrations play a huge role here.

Your cover needs to stand out from the other covers on Amazon. The title should give an idea of what the book is about. A well-placed bold title on the cover also makes it easier for people who scroll through hundreds of thumbnails to notice your book's art and name at a glance.

The rating and the price are also what buyers see before they click on your book.

Seal the deal—convince them of the value of your book.

Once they are on your book page, you have a limited time to convince them that this is the book they are looking for or the book they didn't know they wanted but have to have.

Blurb: Remember, people nowadays have the attention span of a toddler surrounded by old toys. We live in three-second words, and you have that much to grab their attention. No one wants to read a big chunk of text. Separate your blurb into short sections.

I am sure you have seen those sales emails where the text is separated into lines of two or three sentences. Those are well-written copies by professional copywriters. Notice how the small font notices on products or letters are all in one big chunk of text—it's by design with the intention of people not wanting to read them. If you want your blurb to be read, do not put a big chunk of text in front of your potential shoppers.

Begin with a catchy punch line of one sentence. This is the most important line that should make the reader want to know more about the story and the book.

Then, separate the rest of the blurb into small sections. Ensure you have included the benefit for your readers or buyers in that case. Features over content—how your book will benefit them is more important than the story itself.

A+ Content: This is another opportunity to show more of your book. If you have a Board Book or a Picture Book, it is especially useful to show more illustrations. A+ is visual content you can add to your Amazon book's page—images, text, and comparison tables. Think of it as a visual blurb.

Look Inside Feature: Enable the "Look Inside" feature to allow readers to preview a few pages. This feature becomes less important with the rise of the A+ content for books and the ability to send free samples to Kindle, but you can still utilize it.

Reviews and Ratings: We all look at the number of ratings and stars a product has before buying it. Encourage your readers to leave reviews. Include a simple invitation to leave reviews in the back of your book.

Videos: You can upload a book trailer or a different video showcasing your book. Ensure you do not mention Amazon or show the Amazon sign in the video, or it will be declined. Even simple "available on Amazon" will make your video ineligible to be posted.

Author Bio: Include an engaging author bio that builds credibility and connection with readers. Share a bit about yourself, your inspiration, and why you wrote the book.

Chapter 18 Paid Advertising

I know of many successful authors who don't have an active social media presence, but I see their ads on Amazon on a regular basis. Amazon Ads are a great way for children's book authors to reach a wider audience and boost book sales.

Before we dive into the nitty-gritty, let's talk about why you should consider paid advertising. While organic reach on social media and through email marketing is fantastic, paid ads can supercharge your efforts. They will show your book to potential buyers based on your set criteria.

Each type of advertising has its advantages and disadvantages.

Facebook (Meta) and Instagram Ads:

Create and post your ads using the Ads Manager in Meta Business Suite. That gives you the most control over your ad. Perfect for targeting parents and educators. Facebook's robust targeting options allow you to reach exactly the right audience.

You can also Boost posts directly from Instagram or Facebook. Avoid boosting posts from your mobile device. The recently added service charge for IOS users means close to 50% increase in pricing.

Boosted Instagram posts can lead to a sales page, but they are best for gaining new followers and growing your email list.

If you want to sell books, use Facebook Ads Manager to set up your campaigns using exact or wide (my preferred one) targeting and your A/B tests.

Facebook ads run on Instagram and vice versa.

Use *eye-catching images* and write *snappy, engaging text* that piques interest.

Always include a clear Call-to-Action. Tell your audience exactly what you want them to do. "Buy Now," "Learn More," or "Get Your Copy" are clear and effective. Remember, people are more likely to follow instructions when they're not left guessing.

Set Your Budget: Start small, test the waters, and adjust as needed.

Ad Duration: Determine how long you want your ads to run. Short bursts can create urgency, while longer campaigns build sustained awareness. Like baking a cake, timing is everything.

Targeting Your Audience On Facebook and Instagram

Targeting is where the real magic happens. *Or so they say.* Here's how you can narrow down your audience:

Demographics: Start with the basics—age, gender, and location. You'll likely focus on parents, grandparents, and educators for children's books. Picture your ideal reader's parent—*is it the soccer mom, the bookish dad, or the crafty grandma?*

I set my campaigns by narrowing down the audience by *Sex:* women; *Age:* over 25; and *Location:* USA. And I let the bot learn what works for me and what doesn't.

You can also narrow it down by:

Interests and hobbies: Target people who love reading, kids' activities, education, or anything related to your book's theme. It's like aiming a spotlight directly at your target market.

Behaviors: Consider targeting based on behavior, such as purchasing habits or device usage.

I have tried to narrow it down to parents of kids of a certain age, target women who are interested in literacy, or one of the big publishers, and yet had the same success as with the ads where I did NOT narrow the audience down that much. People go to Facebook and Instagram to communicate with friends and check out some new reels. Their initial goal is not shopping.

Regularly monitor and adjust your ads.

Analytics: Use the platform's analytics tools to track impressions, clicks, and conversions.

A/B Testing: Test different versions of your ads to see which ones perform better. Change one element at a time—like the image, headline, or call-to-action—and see what works better.

Adjusting: Don't be afraid to tweak your ads based on performance. If something's not working, change it.

Fear of missing out is real, but remember, professionals are driven by data, not feelings.

Amazon ads:

Amazon is the world's largest online bookstore *(yes, I already mentioned that, but it's important)*, making it the perfect place to advertise your children's books. People visit Amazon with the intention of buying, so your ads are reaching potential customers who are ready to hit that "Buy Now" button.

Running Amazon ads used to be much less expensive, but with the rise of indie publishing, it has become a significant expense. That is why specific targeting and regular monitoring and adjusting are so important.

Here are some of the PROs of Amazon ads:

They give your book a visibility boost.

Ads are triggered by keywords, ensuring your book is shown to readers looking for similar titles. You only pay when someone clicks on your ad, so your budget goes directly toward generating interest.

Some of the CONs:

Amazon ads can be expensive.

They need regular monitoring and adjustment.

It takes time to find profitable targets.

Types of Amazon ads

Amazon offers several types of ads, each with its own unique strengths. Let's break them down so you can choose the best ones for your book.

Sponsored Products ads appear in search results and on product pages, blending seamlessly with organic listings.

Begin by setting up an *automatic campaign* that draws keywords from your metadata.
The beauty of automatic campaigns is that you can check what keywords people search for when they click on an ad or purchase your book. That way, you can determine what keywords work for your book and which are just bleeding you dry.

Next, set up a campaign using relevant *keywords* related to your book. Use the keywords that you find working for your automatic campaign. And think like a parent or educator searching for new reading material. Keywords like "children's books" or "books for kids" are highly competitive, expensive, and less likely to be profitable. Narrowing down your keywords by including age or grade, for example, can be more profitable: "children's bedtime stories for three-year-old girls," "educational books for preschoolers," or "funny children's books for boys" can be more effective than general keywords. Keep an eye on your keyword performance and adjust bids to maximize visibility.

How to find keywords?

Start typing in Amazon's search bar like you would when you search for any other product, and a list of suggestions will drop. Those are phrases that people often search for.

Use *Publisher Rocket* to find and analyze keywords. *Publisher Rocket* is a data-driven tool that helps analyze the competitiveness of keywords, research categories, and check competitors' performance. It also has a very cool feature helping you find relative keywords for your Amazon ads.

Product Targeting: Look for books that are similar to yours and target them. Make sure the books you target have good traffic—look at their Amazon ranking—the lower the number, the better. There is no point in targeting books that have no traffic. Your ad will be shown to no one.

Categories: Since Amazon only allows you to choose three categories per book (for new books) when you set up your title on KDP, here is your chance to show your book in more places.

Sponsored Brands: These ads appear at the top of search results and feature your logo, a custom headline, and multiple products. They are great for authors with multiple books, helping you build a recognizable brand. The prominent placement and custom visuals make these ads hard to miss.

Showcase several of your books simultaneously, perfect for series or thematic collections.

The option to run trailers *(Yay!)* has been a game-changer for me. Now, you have the option to use a video in your Sponsored Brand ad, and in the future, you will be able to feature a single product or lead buyers to your Author page. That has proven very profitable for me. Amazon has not been overwhelmed by video ads yet, and that is why those are less competitive and more profitable right now. I am sure that will change over time.

Create a compelling headline that highlights the unique selling points of your books. Use high-quality images and make sure your logo is clear and professional. Target keywords representing your brand's overall theme and monitor performance to optimize your campaigns.

Setting bid and budget

Amazon ads are Pay-per-Click (PPC) ads. You pay when someone clicks on your ad, not how many people see it. You decide how much you are willing to pay for each keyword, category, or targeted product—that is your bid.

There are different strategies when setting up a campaign.

Low bids: You stuff your ad with many keywords and bid 13-18 cents on each—those used to be more effective before, but not so much now.

Medium bid: 35-45 cents per target. That is a conservative approach for a steady gain.

High bids: >$1 For a fast take-off.

Of course, after adjusting, those bids will change.

You set the number of targets in each ad depending on your bid amount and daily budget for the ad. For example, if you set a daily budget of $5 per campaign and your bid is $0.50, realistically, your budget will be used up after only ten clicks. That is why Amazon will most likely show impressions for only five targets. There is no point in padding an ad with a hundred or more keywords when you have a low budget. Most of my ads have no more than thirty targets, and I use the medium bid approach.

Standard Ad versus Custom Text Ad

Custom Text allows you to include a short blurb with your ad. It's a personal preference—you must test what works for you. I haven't found a difference in performance, so I stick with Standard Ad. In my opinion, people don't stop to read the small text included with your cover.

Dynamic Bids versus Fixed Bids

You can give Amazon the option to reduce or increase your bid depending on "the chance of making a sale." I am a little bit of a control freak and would like to know how much I would spend on an ad. My choice is usually a fixed bid unless I am doing a very aggressive campaign.

Per Amazon: *"Campaigns using 'Dynamic bids—up and down' delivered 1.8x more sales, at a 4% lower ROAS (Return On Ad Spend), compared to campaigns using 'Dynamic bids—down only' (Amazon internal data, 2022)."*

You can also adjust your bid per placement. It's worth to bid for higher placement. The higher your book's search result, the better your chances of making a sale.

Your strategy depends on your budget and how fast you want to take that book of ground.

I prefer to begin running ads after my books have at least twenty (hopefully positive) reviews and have gained some credibility.

Monitoring and Optimizing

Once your ads are live, it's time to monitor and optimize. Keep an eye on key metrics like impressions, clicks, and conversions. Amazon's advertising dashboard provides detailed insights to help you understand what's working.

Adjust your bids based on performance. Increase bids for high-performing keywords and reduce or remove bids for those not delivering.

Do not waste money on keywords you *feel* should work but do not deliver. Again, professionals act based on data, not feelings.

Adjust your campaigns every two weeks. Remember, it can take a day for the new bids to take effect, and Amazon is often late with the reporting.

Paid advertising can seem daunting, but with a bit of strategy, it can be a highly effective way to promote your children's books.

Sometimes, your Amazon ads dashboard does not show many sales, but your KDP dashboard shows earned royalties. Then, you stop an ad, thinking it is not profitable, and your KDP dashboard turns blank. This is the Amazon algorithm at work. Amazon helps books that are selling by showing them to even more readers. Your ad brings a few sales, and Amazon shows your book to even more buyers who then purchase it. So, your Amazon ads bring organic sales that are not reflected on your Ads Console but would not have happened without your ad in the first place. The more your book sells, the more Amazon offers it to buyers looking for similar books.

To judge the profitability of your ads, you need to look at all the sales and not only the ones reflected on your Ads Console.

Chapter 19 Email List

You communicate with your readers on Amazon in a limited and mostly one-sided way. You make your statement through your blurb and bio, and they respond to you through their reviews. There is limited communication but no actual dialogue. Most importantly, you do not have a list of the customers who purchased your book from Amazon.

Facebook groups can be a great way to communicate with your fans, but algorithms often change, and not everyone sees your posts.

Email is your direct line of communication with your readers. You own your email list, which allows you to connect with your readers freely and ensures your message reaches them.

An email list lets you share updates about new releases, events, and special promotions directly with your audience, fostering a loyal fan base. It also provides valuable insights into your readers' preferences, helping you effectively tailor your content and marketing efforts.

I am including a list of the most popular email marketing service providers in the Resources section at the end of the book. When deciding on which one to use, compare their pricing model and the features they offer.

There are different ways to increase your email list. You should include a pop-up box and embedded forms on your website to collect emails and offer a lead magnet—free book, coloring sheets, or lesson plans—to entice people to sign up. On your sign-up forms, explain what your subscribers are getting in exchange for their email—a free book, activity sheets, or maybe classroom resources.

"Let's keep in touch" is very general and not enticing. "A free book and a whole week of activities for your kids" sounds way more attractive. Set the expectation and fulfill it.

A great way to collect emails is to include QR codes with a link to your email list at the end of all your books. Sign up with *Book Funnel* and offer your lead magnet there. Participate in promos with other authors or author swaps. Include a link to a sign-up form on your social media.

Chapter 20 Email Automation and Segmentation

Email Automations are scheduled emails customers receive when a specific action is taken. That can be signing up for your email list or clicking on a link in one of your emails.

Drip Campaigns are a series of automated emails that customers receive once they land on your email list. Use drip campaigns to build that connection with your readers. The beauty of those is that once you set them up, they work for you quietly in the background, without much effort from you.

Begin with a short introduction and a link to download what you promised them for signing up. Tell them what they can expect from you, and thank them for subscribing to your list. Then, in the following email, offer more value connected to your book or expertise.

For my children's books, I have a sequence of ten emails that subscribers receive a few days apart.

Make your newsletter valuable.

Share personal anecdotes or funny stories from your life as an author. Let your personality shine through—humor goes a long way in building connections. Be genuine and a little vulnerable (if you are comfortable with that). Include fun activities, like printable coloring pages, puzzles, or simple DIY crafts related to your books. Share exciting news about your books, upcoming releases, or special events. Take your readers behind the scenes of your writing process. Share photos of your workspace, snippets of your works-in-progress, or your quirky habits while writing. Ask questions or run polls to encourage reader interaction. For example, *"Which character would you like to see in a new adventure?"* or *"Which book made you a reader?"* Run exclusive contests and giveaways for your subscribers.

Email marketing and newsletters are great for connecting with your readers and building a loyal audience. Handled right, those would be the tools that will make you the most sales without actually selling. The rule for email marketing is the same as social media posts: one in five can be promotional. The others need to deliver content your subscribers will find helpful or entertaining. That is called delivering value. The main goal of your newsletter is to create a relationship with your subscribers.

Email marketing is not for selling; it's for building connections and creating superfans.

Chapter 21 Reviews

If you have read my *Roadmap To Publishing Children's Books*, you already know the importance of reviews.

How do you make your selections on Amazon? I look at the ratings and bet you do that, too. Reviews on Amazon give credibility to your book. There are different ways to obtain your initial reviews. But first, here is a note on Amazon Reviews: *Amazon has a very strict policy regarding reviews. You cannot pay for reviews. You cannot swap reviews with other authors or request a certain type of review. You cannot require reviews. You can only encourage your readers to leave honest reviews.*

Launch Team

Your Launch Team is a group of dedicated readers willing to leave reviews in exchange for a free digital book called an Advanced Reader Copy (ARC).

The most common two ways to form a Launch Team are to collect emails through an online form and then email them to your team or create a Facebook page specially for your team and post your updates there.

The Facebook page approach keeps people more involved, but you still have to collect their emails and deliver their advance reading copy as a PDF.

People sign up for Launch Teams because they want to help the author and because they receive a free book in exchange for their help. You can email them a PDF with your book or schedule a free Kindle promotion through KDP. I do both at the same time.

The PDFs I send are typically with a watermark and lower quality than the copies I use for the printers. That way, I can prevent people from stealing my work and publishing it as their own.

Only 10-30% of the people who sign up will leave reviews. If you want twenty reviews, you must have at least fifty people on your team. That's what I aim for.

Email your Launch Team on release day or post in your Facebook group dedicated to your launch.

Send your Advanced Readers Copies out and ask your team to leave their reviews. Once again, you cannot require them to do so, but you can encourage them.

Forming a Launch team serves another purpose as well. Not only do those dedicated readers review your book, but they also share it with their followers, friends, and family. They can be your biggest cheerleaders and help you get the word out.

Next, run your Free Kindle Promo days.

Schedule your Free Kindle Promo in advance. A quick note: your book has to be published before you can schedule a free promo. It cannot be done while the book is on pre-order.

Post about your promotion in groups for authors you have already been active in and have established connections with. Authors help each other but need to see that you're a contributing member of their tribe.

Combining Amazon free promotions with paid promo sites is one of the most effective and fastest ways to gain your first reviews.

Setting Up an Amazon Free Promotion

Amazon's KDP Select program allows you to choose between a countdown deal or a free book promotion. The countdown deal is essentially lowering the price of your Kindle eBook for a few days and is a less effective type of promotion for children's books. Free book, on the other hand, is an excellent way for readers to preview your book before committing to buy the physical version.

Here's how to set it up:

First, ensure your book is enrolled in Amazon's KDP Select program. This gives you the ability to offer your book for free for up to five days every ninety days.

Plan your free promotion dates strategically. Avoid major holidays or busy shopping periods when readers might be distracted by other things. A mid-week promotion can often work better than one running over the weekend.

Before the promotion starts, ensure your book page is polished. Update your book description, make sure your cover is appealing, and add any new reviews or accolades.

Boosting Your Promotion with Paid Promo Sites

To maximize the impact of your free promotion, combine it with paid promo sites that specialize in spreading the word about free eBooks. Here are some steps and tips to get you started.

Research Promo Sites: Look for reputable sites that cater to your target audience. Sites like *Fussy Librarian, The eReader Café, BookBub*, and *Freebooksy* have large followings and can significantly boost your promotion's visibility. *BookBub* has the best subscribers list for free and discounted promos. To be featured in their promo newsletter, you have to be approved. The cost is higher than similar services, but the returns are also much higher.

Look at their readership numbers and pick the ones with an established children's audience.

Services I have used successfully:

The Fussy Librarian
The eReader Café
FreeBooksy
BookBub

Submit your book to these promo sites in advance. Each site will have its own requirements, so follow their guidelines carefully. Highlight any unique features of your book, such as awards, unique themes, or rave reviews.

A note on Amazon algorithm: if you want your Kindle book to stay longer in those sweet higher ranking spots and take advantage of Amazon showing it to more readers, schedule your five free days together. If your book raises in ranking just for a day or two, it will drop back down fast. The longer it stays in the higher ranking, the longer Amazon will keep it there after the promo ends. Amazon's algorithm likes consistency. My advice is to schedule your five days together and book a promo with a different site each day. That way, you will take maximum advantage of your free promo days.

Running the Promotion

When the day of your promotion arrives, it's time to put your plan into action. Spread the word on your social media channels, website, and email newsletter. Make a big deal out of your free promotion—use eye-catching graphics and enthusiastic language to generate excitement.

Encourage your followers and email list to download your book and share the promotion with their friends. A simple,

"Hey, everyone, my book is free today! Grab a copy and let me know what you think!" can go a long way.

Keep an eye on your download numbers throughout the promotion. This will help you gauge the effectiveness of your paid promos and make adjustments if necessary.

Once readers have your book in their hands, the next step is to encourage them to leave reviews. Here's how to do it without sounding desperate:

At the end of your book, include a polite request for a review. Something like, *"Thank you for reading! If you enjoyed this story, please consider leaving a review on Amazon. Your feedback helps other readers discover my book."*

If you have an email list, send a follow-up email a week or two after the promotion. Remind your subscribers about the free download and gently ask for reviews. A friendly note like, *"I hope you enjoyed [Book Title]! Reviews are incredibly helpful for indie authors like me—if you have a moment, I'd love to hear your thoughts on Amazon,"* can be effective.

Use your social media platforms to remind readers to leave reviews. Share snippets of positive feedback you've already received (with permission) to show that you value reader reviews.

Leveraging Reviews for Continued Success

Once you start accumulating reviews, use them to promote your book further.

Update Your Book Page: Highlight positive reviews on your Amazon book page and in your book description.

Share on Social Media: Create visually appealing graphics featuring snippets of glowing reviews and share them on social media.

Combining Amazon free promotions with paid promo sites is a potent strategy for generating reviews and boosting your book's visibility. By carefully planning your promotion, engaging with your audience, and encouraging reviews, you can create a buzz around your book, leading to long-term success.

Trade Reviews

Trade reviews from esteemed publications like *Kirkus Reviews* and *Library Journal* are highly respected within the industry. They often influence librarians, booksellers, and educators in purchasing decisions. A positive review from *Kirkus, School Library Journal,* or *Publishers Weekly* lends credibility and significantly enhances your book's visibility. However, these reviews can be challenging to secure and sometimes come with a fee, especially for indie authors.

Submit your books for a chance to be chosen for a free review, but with the benefits of the paid services offered. If your book's primary market is not libraries, you don't need to pay for those services. Most online buyers do not know what a trade review is, nor do they care.

Chapter 22 A Word on Book Awards

Being an award-winning author sounds so cool.

Not all awards are created equal, though. Some prestigious awards, such as the Newbery Medal or the Caldecott Medal, carry significant clout and can greatly enhance your book's credibility and sales. On the other hand, many lesser-known or pay-to-win awards might sound impressive but offer little real value. These can sometimes be more about profit for the organizers than recognition for genuine literary merit.

When considering entering your book for awards, research thoroughly to ensure the accolade will help you and isn't just a shiny but a hollow praise.

A seal on your cover might seem cool, but buyers are not looking for seals, and those have little to no input into their purchase decisions. I recommend spending your money elsewhere because awards don't usually translate to sales.

Do your research and apply for prestigious awards instead of jumping into every contest for a fee that has no value to you or your potential customers.

REFLECTION

As you reach the end of this book, it's time to reflect on your journey so far and take stock of what you've learned. Now is the moment to assess your successes, acknowledge any challenges, and create an action plan for moving forward. Below, I am sharing my own mistakes to help you avoid those pitfalls and make your path smoother. Remember to pace yourself and set realistic goals to avoid burnout— building a successful author career is a marathon, not a sprint.

Chapter 23 My Mistakes

My biggest mistake: for the launch of *Mother's Love*, **I hired a "Publicity company."** I didn't do my due diligence, and even though it was apparent their Instagram account was full of fake followers, I made excuses for them, with them being new and having to start from somewhere. I wanted it to work so badly that I went blind to all the glaring red signs; like their books having no reviews and not selling at all. Five thousand dollars later, it was my worst launch ever. I'm not sure how many authors they swindled, but I bet it was quite a few before they renamed themselves and continued to do the same. As far as I can tell, no publicity company can do wonders for indie children's book authors.

Thanks to that mistake, I learned how to do my marketing properly myself.

Being Afraid to Put Myself Out There

For a long time, I was afraid to put myself out there. I hesitated to share my work, promote my books, or even talk about my projects. My friends believed in me more than I believed in myself, and their encouragement was often the only thing that pushed me forward. This fear held me back from reaching my full potential and connecting with a broader audience.

Believe in yourself and your work. Putting yourself out there is scary, but it's necessary for growth and success. Trust your abilities and don't be afraid to share your passion with the world.

Even though, I am still skittish when it comes to in-person events, I developed my way of connecting with my audience digitally.

On and off marketing

Another major mistake was my inconsistent marketing efforts. Marketing is crucial for any author, but especially for indie authors. I fell into the trap of starting and stopping my marketing campaigns, which cost me both time and money. Each time I paused, I had to start from scratch to rebuild momentum, which was incredibly frustrating and inefficient.

Consistency is vital in marketing. Develop a sustainable marketing plan that you can stick to over the long haul. Even if modest, regular marketing efforts are far more effective than sporadic, intensive campaigns.

Fear of missing out

I have spent a lot of money delivering ads to people who were not interested in my books out of fear that I might miss a sale. That applies to Facebook and Instagram ads and Amazon Ads. Nowadays, I try to make decisions based on data instead of feelings.

Not adjusting Amazon Ads

Leaving Amazon Ads to run without evaluating them and adjusting them regularly can bleed you a lot of money.

Hiring others to run my Facebook and Amazon Ads Make

sure to express your expectations clearly. Everyone can spend money running your ads, but not everyone can be profitable.

I have, in the past, hired others to handle different aspects of my marketing. The problem with that was that, in most cases, those freelancers could not deliver anything different than what I could do myself, and they were not even invested in the success of my books.

I am not suggesting you try to do it all yourself, but do your due diligence and not hire someone just because you *want it to work*. Most freelancers in this business are authors themselves. Checking how their own books are doing is the fastest way to evaluate their skills.

After these costly mistakes, I realized that no one would care about my books as much as I did. I set out to learn how to market my own books myself because I wanted control over my success. That doesn't mean to never let someone handle different aspects of your marketing; just make sure you do your homework before hiring them.

Mistakes are inevitable in any career, but they are also our greatest teachers. By sharing my experiences, I hope to help other authors navigate the complex world of publishing and marketing more easily and confidently. Remember, it's okay to make mistakes—as long as you learn from them and use those lessons to grow and improve.

Chapter 24 Avoid Burnout

Trying to manage every aspect of digital media in a frenzy can lead to quick burnout. Take it from me; I have been there many times.

You need a plan that will give you time to have a successful and consistent campaign and give you a break at the same time.

I like to take one week of the month and prepare and schedule all my content and have the rest of the month for writing and other parts of my life.

You either learn to love it and give yourself a break when needed, or you have to hire someone else to do certain aspects of the work while you track the results. Hiring specialists to manage your social media or create marketing materials (as you should if you are not a graphic designer in training, at least) can save valuable time and ensure these tasks are handled expertly. However, it's crucial to choose professionals who come highly recommended. Trustworthy referrals from fellow authors or industry connections can help you find reliable, skilled individuals who will treat your book's promotion with the same care and passion you do. Make a plan of action and stick to it.

Persistence and consistency are the keys to success in the publishing business!

By understanding the intricacies of book marketing, I could ensure that my efforts were genuine and targeted. This journey was challenging but ultimately rewarding. It empowered me to take my career into my own hands and build a direct connection with my readers.

I hope you find this book helpful.
Marketing is not about your story. It's about your customers' needs. You don't sell a book. You fulfill a need or solve a problem.

How do you accomplish that?
You need to know your book, story, message, theme...
You need to understand your customers.
You will get the best results if you combine all the avenues and tools mentioned in this book. They all work together to complete each other's efforts, turning all aspects of your marketing into a well-oiled machine.

Seeing the full impact of your marketing efforts doesn't happen overnight. Every little step you take builds on the last, and with time and consistency, momentum grows. Small, steady actions lead to measurable success in increasing your visibility, deepening engagement, and ultimately achieving the growth you've worked toward. Keep building—every effort counts toward your long-term success.

RESOURCES

For ready-to-use templates that can help with your marketing journey, visit https://www.dedonibooks.com/resources

Check out THE INDIE CHILDREN'S BOOK AUTHOR on Patreon for the latest on Writing, Publishing, and Marketing.

https://www.patreon.com/dedonibooks

Amazon Ads Academy

https://advertising.amazon.com/academy

Analytics:

https://analytics.google.com/

https://www.hootsuite.com

https://www.notjustanalytics.com

https://www.facebook.com/ads/library

https://clicky.com

https://usefathom.com

Book description generator and a QR generator:

https://kindlepreneur.com

Content Creation:

https://www.canva.com – Graphics and Videos

https://placeit.net - Mockups

https://elevenlabs.io - AI Voice Over

Email marketing services:

https://mailchimp.com

https://www.mailerlite.com

https://convertkit.com

https://www.authoremail.com

Freelance sites:

https://reedsy.com

https://www.upwork.com

https://www.fiverr.com

https://www.freelancer.com

File distribution and email collection:

https://bookfunnel.com

Keywords, Categories, and Competitors Research:

https://publisherrocket.com

Linktree: Social media reference page. Allows you to create a landing page with different links.

https://linktr.ee

Press release distribution:

https://www.send2press.com

https://www.newswire.com

Promo Sites:

https://www.thefussylibrarian.com

https://theereadercafe.com

https://www.freebooksy.com

https://www.bookbub.com

Social Media Content Scheduling Tool:

https://buffer.com

https://www.hootsuite.com

https://sproutsocial.com

Website-building platforms:

https://www.wix.com

https://www.squarespace.com

https://www.weebly.com

https://wordpress.com

https://www.shopify.com

https://www.godaddy.com

If you found this book helpful, please take a moment and

leave a review on Amazon or Goodreads!

Your feedback is deeply appreciated!